CAREERS IN

STATE, COUNTY, AND CITY POLICE FORCES

CAREERS IN

STATE, COUNTY, AND CITY POLICE FORCES

BY ADAM WOOG

Cavendish Square

New York

To my daughter, Leah, who inspired this book and still inspires me

ACKNOWLEDGMENTS

My thanks to these men and women for sharing their time and expertise:
Officer Adam Elias, Seattle (Washington) Police Department
Sergeant J. J. Gundermann, Washington State Patrol
Trooper Shelley Izzard, Michigan State Police
Dispatcher Leslie Lugo, Dutchess County (New York) Sheriff's Office
Senior Officer Mike McCoy, Houston (Texas) Police Department
Deputy Sheriff David D. Peterson, Benton County (Oregon) Sheriff's Office
Officer Jennifer Williamson, Orange County (Florida) Sheriff's Office.

With special thanks to Carlos Perea, academic advisor for the
Department of Criminology and Criminal Justice at University of Maryland, College Park.

Published in 2014 by Cavendish Square Publishing, LLC
303 Park Avenue South, Suite 1247, New York, NY 10010

Copyright © 2014 by Cavendish Square Publishing, LLC

First Edition

LIBRARY OF CONGRESS CATALOGING-IN-PUBLICATION DATA

Woog, Adam, 1953-
Careers in State, County, and City Police Forces / Adam Woog.
p. cm. — (Law and Order jobs.)
Includes bibliographical references and index.
ISBN 978-1-62712-425-6 (hardcover) ISBN 978-1-62712-426-3 (paperback) ISBN 978-1-62712-427-0 (ebook)
1. Police—Vocational guidance—Juvenile literature. 2. Law enforcement—Vocational guidance—Juvenile literature. I. Title. HV7922.W66 2014 363.2023—dc23 2011022543

ART DIRECTOR: Anahid Hamparian   SERIES DESIGNER: Michael Nelson
LAYOUT DESIGN: Joseph Macri   EDITOR: Dean Miller
Photo research by Marybeth Kavanaugh
The photographs in this book are used by permission and through the courtesy of: Cover photo by 2009 © David Bacon / The Image Works. © The Star Ledger/John O'Boyle / The Image Works, 4-5; © Ronnie Kaufman/Corbis, 8; © David M. Grossman/The Image Works, 12; © Newscom/ZUMA Press, 15; © Stock Connection Blue/Alamy, 26; © Peter Hvizdak/The Image Works, 30; © AP Images/John Harrell, 33; © AP Images/Daily Progress, Matt Gentry, 38; © John Davenport/San Antonio Express-News/ZUMA Press, 41; ©Bryan Smith/ZUMA Press., 43; Spencer Platt/Collection/Getty Images, 47; © Spencer Grant/PhotoEdit Inc., 50; © Bob Daemmrich/ The Image Works, 61; Photo by Richard A. Lipski/The Washington Post/Getty Images, 69; © 2008 Roll Call Photos, 70; ©Bob Daemmrich/The Image Works, 79; © AP Images/Toby Talbot, 81.

Printed in the United States of America

CONTENTS

INTRODUCTION

MAKING THE WORLD A BETTER PLACE

"ONCE, ON A TRAFFIC STOP," MICHIGAN STATE Trooper Shelley Izzard recalls, "I saw the driver slam his hands down and toss his head back and forth like he was ticked off at the police." She goes on,

> When I [spoke with] him, I could tell he was having problems, both personally and financially. I treated him with complete respect and dignity, no need to go "tough guy" on him. That's not what the job is about.
>
> I didn't write him a ticket. I gave him a verbal warning and suggested the things he needed to get fixed on his car. And I got a "Thank you very much ma'am, you have yourself a good night and be safe." By the time we were done, you could tell his entire perception of police had changed.

Trooper Izzard understands well that someone who comes into contact with a law enforcement officer—or with someone whose job is to support that officer—probably is not having a great day. Police officers, and those who work with them, frequently encounter deadly car accidents, child abuse, and violent crime. And they routinely see people at their worst, whether those people are breaking a law or in some kind of distress. Sergeant J. J. Gundermann of the Washington State Patrol comments:

> It can be frustrating because 90% of the people we come in contact with are at their worst. You deal with career criminals, and then you see good people who make mistakes [or are upset]. It's hard when you become part of other peoples' tragedies.
>
> [But] it does make a difference when you're out there in the pouring rain and you come up on somebody who's got a flat tire and two kids in the car and they don't know what to do. [Then you realize] you can make a difference—big or small, you're helping them get on their way. It's good to be part of that.

People in law enforcement are frequently given chances to change the lives of others—or to save those lives. Every day, law enforcement professionals have a chance to do something good for the communities they serve. As a result, law enforcement agencies typically create their own mottos and sets of professional standards. The wording of these mission

Every day, police officers do good in the communities they serve.

statements changes from organization to organization, but the basic message is the same: Law enforcement officers and personnel are dedicated to upholding the law and protecting, serving, and improving their communities.

Clearly, a career with a law enforcement agency is multi-faceted. It is challenging and exciting work that is guaranteed to keep you on your toes—you won't be doing the same thing every day. There is also room for advancement, which translates to more interesting work and better pay. Of course, there is always the knowledge that you are playing a vital role in keeping your community safe.

WHERE YOU WORK

Broadly speaking, there are three categories of local law enforcement agencies. They cover three general geographic areas: cities, counties, and states. The name of a specific agency indicates the region it serves. City police are responsible for towns and cities. County deputy sheriffs cover counties, which are areas that are not **incorporated**. State troopers are responsible for entire states.

There is often some overlap in the responsibilities of these three levels. For instance, in some cases state troopers enforce the law in small towns or rural areas that do not have the resources or the need to maintain their own police departments. Also, officers from two or more levels of law enforcement, such as a city police force and the FBI, will often work jointly on cases that are better solved by a cooperative effort.

If you are interested in a job with a law enforcement

agency on one of these levels, the chances are good that you will find one. It is unfortunate but true that the need to combat crime is constant. As a result, good officers are always in demand. So are the support staff workers, such as dispatchers and crime scene technicians, who back up those officers.

Whether you are a **sworn officer** or an employee of an agency's support staff, your job will depend on many things. One very important factor is your personal preference—that is, what kind of job you want. For example, you may want to be a patrol officer, or you may be more interested in using your photographic skills to record crime scenes.

Naturally, another factor will be the job openings at the time you apply and how those jobs relate to your preference about where you want to be. For example, you may like the relatively peaceful environment of a small town or a sparsely populated county. You might want to live in a state with abundant wilderness, where you can easily ski or hike. On the other hand, you may crave the excitement and variety of a big city.

NEVER A DULL MOMENT

No matter where you work, one thing is certain: life in a law enforcement agency will rarely be routine. Although there are always some boring but necessary tasks, such as filling out paperwork, dull office routines take up little time.

Mike McCoy, a senior officer in the Houston, Texas, Police Department, comments about a typical shift, "Eight hours can be up before you even know it." Trooper Izzard adds,

You're driving into work and thinking, "Okay, I need to do this or that, follow up with this person or that one, go look for this person because he's dodging me and he knows he's got a warrant for his arrest."

So you want to do all this, and then you walk in the door and you've got a serious traffic crash waiting for you, or a criminal complaint waiting for you, and things change and you have to be able to shift on the fly.

I think that variety, and that need to change gears quickly, really do lure certain people to the job. If you can do that well, then this is a good job for you.

However, a love of variety and fast action, as well as a strong commitment to helping people, are only some of the qualities you'll need to become a law enforcement officer. There are many others. Notably, you'll need a good personal record. That record will include such factors as an arrest-free history, no evidence of regular drug use, a good character, and a certain amount of education. (The amount varies from agency to agency. Some require a college degree, some only a high school diploma or **GED** equivalent.) And, especially if you want to be an officer, you'll need intelligence, bravery, and physical fitness. If you have these qualifications, then it's time to start exploring a career in law enforcement.

Police departments often go into city neighborhoods like this one in Brooklyn to find recruits.

ONE

WHAT IT TAKES:
APPLYING FOR A JOB IN LAW ENFORCEMENT

LONG BEFORE YOU ACTUALLY APPLY FOR A JOB in law enforcement, there are many things to consider and do. These activities will give you a real taste of what it is like to be on the job. For instance, many agencies offer opportunities for ride-alongs—that is, accompanying officers on a shift and observing them as they make their rounds.

These ride-alongs come with strict rules of conduct. Typically, you will have to stay in the patrol car at all times and obey all instructions from the officers, who will never put you in danger. You will wear regular clothes with a jacket clearly marking you as being connected to the officers. Some agencies require that you sign confidentiality agreements, in which you promise not to reveal to others specific details of what you see. The minimum age for going on a ride-along varies from agency to agency, but is generally in the range of fourteen to eighteen years. For instance, the Portland, Oregon, police force sets the minimum age for riding along in one of its vehicles at sixteen.

Making an appointment to talk to a law enforcement recruiter is also helpful. When people are close to graduating from high school or college, recruiters typically help them decide which type of law enforcement, if any, is right for each individual. However, any recruiter would also be happy to talk to younger students about a career in law enforcement.

STUDENT ACADEMIES

A more intensive option is to enroll in one of the annual student programs that many agencies offer. These mini-academies are typically scheduled to run during summer breaks for high school students. They let teenagers experience firsthand the demands, responsibilities, and rewards of police work.

In addition to offering hands-on experience, student academies benefit participants in other ways. For example, attendees can typically apply the time spent at an academy toward required hours of community service.

Furthermore, attending an academy is a good way to make sure that you're noticed by recruiters for future consideration. If you are already an outstanding athlete or a computer whiz, for instance, you can demonstrate your abilities to people who might be looking at your application a few years down the road. In other words, you will be on their radar.

If you attend a summer academy, you will go through many of the programs designed for actual police trainees. For example, you will experience intense physical training, attend classes on a variety of law-related subjects, ride in patrol cars, talk to seasoned police officers, and observe officers assigned to specialty units, such as tactical, major crimes, and **K-9** teams.

A number of law enforcement agencies also participate in programs for high school and college students during the school year. They focus on the work of patrol officers and many other aspects of law enforcement, including probation officers and correctional (jail and prison) officers. In addition to city, county, and state organizations, many military and federal agencies offer similar programs.

These Explorer programs, as they are called, give enrollees firsthand experience in such areas as leadership, marksmanship, the proper use of equipment, and procedures for accidents and other critical situations. Deputy David D. Peterson of the Benton County (Oregon) Sheriff's Office spent at least ten hours a week as an Explorer during high school. He comments, "[Y]ou get to learn about the career, to go on ride-alongs, to volunteer your time for many different kinds of community events."

You can find out more about the Explorer program at the site of the agency that runs national Explorer programs: http://exploring.learningforlife.org/services/career-exploring/law-enforcement/

Sheriff's Explorer Lee Harrington uses the loudspeaker on a sheriff's cruiser to order someone out of his car during a mock felony traffic stop drill as part of the Explorer program.

Meanwhile, many city police departments offer a Citizen Police Academy (CPA). These programs, which are typically open to all ages, are designed to involve residents in community-based crime prevention, to let them voice their concerns about police work, to give them an understanding of the criminal justice system and the day-to-day work of real cops (as opposed to how they are portrayed in the media), and to provide information that will help citizens take action on their own to avoid becoming victims of crime.

Police personnel typically conduct classes. Among the topics covered are investigations, explosives, hostage negotiations, firearms, self-defense, narcotics, crime scenes, street gangs, parking policies, and traffic stops. Tours of police facilities, jails, 911 centers, and juvenile detention centers are also program features.

STAYING OUT OF TROUBLE

Even before you are eligible for CPA programs, you can start on the road to a career in law enforcement. In fact, recruiters and others in the field say that it is never too soon. This is equally true if you are interested in becoming a patrol officer or a member of an agency's support staff.

Why is it never too soon to start preparing? Because what you do as a young person can affect your chances of being eligible later in life. Law enforcement agencies will not accept just anyone into their ranks. They are looking for people whose past actions show that they are responsible individuals with histories of public service and good behavior. Conversely, anyone with a history of problems, especially with the law, risks being weeded out during the application process.

So what can students do to improve their chances of being accepted? Virtually everyone in law enforcement will give you advice that boils down to a simple, three-word phrase: Use your head.

In other words, get good grades. Be a good citizen. Involve yourself in community activities and volunteer work to show that you have an interest in helping others. Stay away from drugs and alcohol. Go to college if you plan on being promoted down the line.

Above all, stay out of trouble. Senior Officer McCoy of the Houston PD (Police Department) comments, "It's very simple: try to do the right thing. It's not always possible—there'll be times when you're in the wrong place at the wrong time, or you're going to fall for peer pressure. We can overlook some things, but . . . just don't do stupid stuff."

"Stupid stuff" generally means racking up a history of scrapes with the law or at school. A history of such problems, or even such questionable habits as collecting a string of speeding tickets, can weaken your chances of acceptance. A conviction for a felony (serious) crime will automatically disqualify you. (Felons cannot legally carry firearms in the United States.) However, many agencies will not automatically reject you because of a misdemeanor (lesser crime) conviction. These agencies decide such cases on an individual basis, although some require that you have no criminal record for the ten years before you apply.

Some agencies are very strict about an applicant's history,

insisting that a candidate have virtually no previous problems. Those that review applications on a case-by-case basis, however, consider factors like age when a person got into trouble, the seriousness of the crime, and the influence of peer pressure.

DRUGS AND THE INTERNET

The use of drugs or alcohol by minors is often, but not always, cause for disqualification. Beyond this, any agency will require that you be drug-free for a certain number of years prior to applying. Obviously, any agency will also require you to remain drug-free during the application process and afterward.

The way you present yourself publicly, especially on social networking sites, can also affect your chances of acceptance. In other words, your online presence now can have a significant impact down the road. Jennifer Williamson, a school resource officer in the Orlando, Florida, police department, notes that background checks on applicants are very thorough and can go back many years. These background checks include looking at an applicant's pages on social networking sites. Officer Williamson comments:

> A big part of my job in the last year or two has been dealing with students' responsibilities on the Internet: cyber-bullying, threatening each other or their schools, and what they do on social networking sites. . . .
>
> [So] be very careful what you put on the Internet. . . . If you portray yourself on the Internet as a thug or a drunk or something because you think it's cool, they [recruiters] are going to find that stuff. . . .

If you put up a picture of yourself, even in middle school, indicating that you're a gang member, our gang units are monitoring that stuff and they're going to label you. And that's the end of your job as a cop, because you got that label when you were twelve and established a reputation for yourself.

That's our recruiting section's biggest nightmare right now, trying to get people who haven't portrayed themselves negatively online."

QUALIFICATIONS

As you get close to graduating from high school, or later from college, you can start getting ready to begin your formal application process. The first step is to decide which agencies you will apply to.

The websites of these agencies may list job openings. They also provide information about the minimum standards required for those jobs. Although requirements will vary depending on the specific job and the specific agency, some rules tend to be similar from place to place.

One important minimum prerequisite is an age requirement. Usually, the youngest an applicant can be is eighteen, although some agencies accept no one under the age of twenty-one. Also, you must be a U.S. citizen. Military service is not necessary, but it is definitely a plus. Furthermore, you will need an e-mail address and phone number, so that the agency can contact you while the application is being processed. And, except for some support jobs, you must have a valid driver's license.

As for education, some law enforcement agencies require a college degree—either an associate degree (from a two-year institution, such as a community college) or a bachelor's degree (from a four-year university). However, some agencies do not require a college degree at all. They require only a high school diploma or GED.

No matter how high you go in your studies, having a well-rounded and practical education is important. Washington State Patrol Sergeant J. J. Gundermann points out that much of a law enforcement officer's job requires general knowledge in such areas as math and physics. This is true because these skills are often needed to handle tasks such as analyzing traffic accidents. He comments, "You've got to have some math to be a trooper. I wish my math teacher had told me that in high school!"

SHOULD I STUDY CRIMINAL JUSTICE?

It is widely thought that a college degree in criminal justice and criminology is a good way to prepare for a career in the field. In many ways, this is indeed a big help, and many professionals suggest it as a sensible and useful major.

However, it is not required, and not everyone agrees that it is the best route. One such person is Deputy Sheriff David Peterson in the Benton County Sheriff's Office. Deputy Peterson himself has a bachelor's degree in criminal justice, but he feels that there are other paths to take:

> It does give you a lot of information about theories about crime. But does that directly translate into your day-to-day work? Not really. The reason you need a college degree is that's the way you advance into

management. But . . . in management, a lot of what they do is spend time with budgets. So you might do better to get a degree in business or accounting.

Also, if you have a business degree or something, you have a backup plan and can do another job. There's a high burnout rate to being an officer, so if that happens, or if you get injured, you have a backup job. I wish someone had given me that advice in high school.

Many law enforcement professionals stress that you need more than just classroom learning. Having a variety of life experiences is also important. Officer Adam Elias of the Seattle Police Department comments on this point:

The biggest thing I think is to diversify. [Recruiters] want to see people who have done sports, been in the military or volunteered in high school, or have had other jobs or honor society or extracurricular activity.

I can't generalize, but in Seattle . . . basically we look for people with life experiences, not necessarily someone who's straight out of college who has never really done anything in life. Because when you get thrown into these situations [on the street] you have to have some experience to fall back on.

THE NEXT STEP

If you meet the basic requirements for education, age, background, and other areas, you can then go on to fill out an application. Most agencies are set up to allow you to apply online.

Typically, the application form will ask for a lot of details about your life, such as information about your school and work experience. You will probably also be asked to write a short essay about why you want to become a law enforcement officer.

The agency will examine this application carefully. Then, if you meet the basic criteria, you'll be scheduled for a series of written and physical tests.

Be forewarned, though: from here on in, things will be increasingly difficult. Only a small fraction of applicants will pass even the first tests. Officer McCoy comments, "One out of twenty people who apply to be a Houston police officer, and I'm sure it's similar around the country, meet the criteria."

The details of the testing process vary from one agency to another. However, the basics are the same: physical testing, written and oral exams, and background checks.

Smaller agencies often have testing periods for potential officers only at certain times of the year, such as one testing period every six months. However, some large agencies schedule these periods all year round. For example, the Los Angeles Police Department schedules the written part of its test several times a week. Typically, if you fail, you can reapply and repeat the exam at the next scheduled test period. It's a little different for support staff. Typically, agencies will advertise (on their websites and elsewhere) available positions as they come up.

PHYSICAL TESTS

The physical fitness part of the testing process can be crucial. Of course, this does not necessarily apply to a support staff position that is primarily a desk job, such as a lab technician or a dispatcher (also called a telecommunicator, the person who receives emergency calls and coordinates the movements of officers in the field). In the case of physical disability, agencies follow standard federal hiring regulations, which are specified in the Americans with Disabilities Act of 1990.

If you're hoping to be an officer, you'll need to be in excellent condition. After all, to perform well in many dangerous situations, you'll need speed, stamina, and strength. Furthermore, officers are sometimes required to put in long hours with little rest, so the ability to stay alert is also important. Additionally, a candidate cannot have vision or hearing problems serious enough to interfere with the job.

It should be no surprise that the physical testing phase of the application process for officers is a tough one. Typically, this means completing such tests as a minimum number of sit-ups and push-ups, or running a track or obstacle course within a set amount of time. The requirements for female applicants are slightly different from those for male applicants. For example, they are typically allowed to perform fewer push-ups than men, and they have more time in which to complete runs. Nonetheless, the physical requirements for women are extremely rigorous.

Many applicants do not get past this part of the testing process. For example, the Oregon State Patrol estimates that just the push-ups and sit-ups portions of its initial testing eliminate around half the candidates.

If you pass the basic fitness tests, you will next be asked to undergo a medical examination. A doctor will check your overall health records and test factors such as your eyesight, hearing, and reflexes. Some agencies are stricter than others about minimum medical requirements. For example, the police force in Tallahassee, Florida, has a rule that its officers must be nonsmokers—both on and off duty.

Because the fitness portion of the test is so rigorous, recruiters often encourage candidates to begin a personal training regimen before submitting their applications. Some agencies offer special pretesting programs that will help you prepare. The Los Angeles Police Department offers a four-month preapplication fitness program that focuses on developing potential applicants' fitness through such techniques as flexibility exercises, strength training, endurance runs, calisthenics, and self-defense techniques.

Recruiters in the past sometimes found that women were concerned that they wouldn't be accepted by a law enforcement agency because of the physical requirements. However, any recruiter will tell you that physical strength is not the most important consideration—or even an important consideration at all. As a result, more and more women are entering the field. Trooper Izzard provides an updated perspective:

> It used to be a man's world. But you need women on the road. . . .
>
> You don't need to go in and muscle everybody—you need to go in and be smart. You have to use your head—this is not a job where brawn wins all the time, this is where you think things through and you talk and reason with people. I know I'm not going to get

PHYSICAL TESTS FOR FEMALE V. MALE APPLICANTS

Physical fitness is crucial to successful police work, and all agencies require applicants to meet certain minimum limits. The fitness requirements are so daunting that some women may be reluctant to take the test. However, more and more women want to join agencies, and agencies have become increasingly interested in recruiting them. As a result, some aspects of these tests have been modified. The intent is to accurately reflect the physical abilities that women will need to have on the job.

For example, the Phoenix, Arizona, Police Department's testing for applicants between twenty and twenty-nine years old requires, for a run of 1.5 miles [2.4 kilometers (km)], a minimum time of 11:58 minutes for men and 14:15 minutes for women. For sit-ups within one minute, men must be able to do at least forty and women thirty-five. For push-ups the minimum for men is thirty-three, while for women it is eighteen.

into a throw-down with a six-foot-four, 300-pound person—that's not smart for anyone. I've got to think and talk and give and get respect.

OTHER TESTS AND BACKGROUND CHECKS

Assuming that you pass the physical testing, the next step in the process involves a series of written and oral exams. These typically cover both general knowledge of the world and more specific knowledge of laws and police procedures. Many of these tests, or ones like them, will also be required of applicants for other positions within the agency.

One of the most important aspects of the written test is to assess a candidate's reading and writing skills. Paperwork such as report filing is an important part of virtually every position in law enforcement. So it is crucial that officers and other personnel be able to write concisely and clearly, with proper grammar, vocabulary, and spelling.

The written exams are also opportunities for the department to assess your attention to details. It is important to get right small details such as factual information, spelling, and punctuation. Officer McCoy emphasizes this point: "Pay attention when you fill out your application. Spell it right! . . . Otherwise it's just pure laziness. Remember—that application's going to be read by everybody up to the chief of police."

In addition to these written tests, candidates in various positions will undergo a series of oral tests and interviews, usually with members of the force. Most agencies also require a **polygraph test**.

If you want to become a law enforcement officer, be prepared to take a polygraph test.

Furthermore, you will be given mental health exams. These will ensure that you have psychological characteristics that fit you to the job. Your general character, personality, emotional stability, and decision-making capabilities will be assessed. This is especially important for potential officers, since they will be handling a variety of problems that require quick decisions—sometimes within seconds.

Other positions require especially sharp skills in specific areas. Although above-average physical strength isn't necessary for everyone, corrections officers, who must be physically strong and unafraid to confront belligerent prisoners, are an obvious exception. Another example concerns dispatchers: the men and women who take calls from the public must decide what course of action to take, find the officers who can respond the fastest, and keep frustrated, frightened, incoherent, or injured callers on the line—all at the same time. Clearly, a good dispatcher has to multitask quickly and intelligently while keeping a cool head.

The mental health tests performed during this phase of the process will also measure your ability to get along with others. Everyone in law enforcement, from patrol officers to secretarial staff, interacts every day with many different kinds of people, both in the force and in the community. So you need a high level of tolerance, patience, and compassion. You also need to be able to work well as part of a team. On the other hand, you need to be comfortable working solo on occasion and capable of making decisions on your own.

While testing is going on, the agency will conduct a background check on you. Recruiters will examine such issues as your financial records, education, prior job experience, and possible drug use; and they will determine whether you have a criminal record of any kind. The agency will also interview family members, friends, neighbors, classmates, work associates, and others—in short, anyone who can provide insights about you and your personality. If this background check reveals any serious problems—or shows that you have lied on your application—you will be immediately disqualified.

RECRUITING

Typically, there are far more applicants than there are available positions in an agency. So anything that sets you apart from other candidates will help your chances of being chosen.

For example, many agencies need officers and other personnel who are fluent in languages besides English. Language skills can be an extremely valuable asset when you are applying for a job. Leslie Lugo, a dispatcher with the Dutchess County (New York) Sheriff's Office, comments, "Definitely if you're bilingual it's a plus. I speak Spanish and so I'm used a lot in our department, translating for people. It's wonderful to be able to do that."

Another thing to consider in the application process is that agencies are far more willing to accept women as officers than in times past, when only positions for support employees were open to women. Things are changing, but the change is slow. As of early 2011, women accounted for only about 13 percent of law enforcement officers nationwide.

Just as women have become increasingly present in law enforcement, so have ethnic and racial minorities. For example, in 1999, minorities made up only 32.6 percent of the New York City Police Department's officers, and only a tiny percentage of its higher-ranked officers, such as captains and inspectors. As of early 2011, however, nearly 53 percent of the NYPD's patrol officers were black, Latino, or Asian. This brings the department closer than ever before in line with the diverse makeup of the city it protects.

Despite efforts by many agencies to actively recruit minority candidates, however, progress nationwide has been uneven. For example, when the city of Harrisburg, Pennsylvania, undertook a concerted effort to recruit minorities into the ranks of its police department, the applicants were nearly all white. Mayor Stephen R. Reed commented at the time, "We are frustrated, surprised, and very disappointed at there not having been minority and female applicants on the top of the civil service list."

SUPPORT STAFF

All law enforcement agencies need staff members, sometimes called civilian or nonsworn employees, who are part of an agency's support service. Support jobs might not be as glamorous as those of troopers, police officers, or deputies, but they are essential. They are also good spots for people beginning their careers, since the knowledge and experience a member of the support staff can gain will be helpful stepping-stones toward becoming a sworn officer.

Lists of available support positions can be found on the websites of individual agencies. If you are willing to relocate, you can also visit one of several sites that list openings nationwide. One such site is allpolicejobs.us.

The many support jobs available within the overall category of local law enforcement range from office staff and lab technicians to jail personnel, parking enforcers, and professionals, such as **evidence technicians**, who work at crime scenes.

PHOTOGRAPHY AND CORRECTIONS

Police photographer is an example of a job that has fairly specific requirements. Broadly speaking, education and experience are key. This might mean a postsecondary education (that is, past high school) in photography or a related field, and/or experience, such as a few years of previous photo work.

To be considered a professional photographer, you'll need not only experience but proof that you've kept up with advances in photo technology and techniques, and willingness to improve your skills all the time.

Police photographers have all kinds of assignments, including taking forensic evidence photographs at crime scenes such as this one in Connecticut.

Furthermore, basic knowledge in certain areas of science and math will be a plus. This is because photos are often used to establish important factors such as position and distance in crime scenes. So, knowledge of geometry and optics is needed to accurately judge angles, perspective, and so on.

On the other hand, to be hired for other support positions, such as correctional officer, you typically will need a less specific skill set. Correctional officers work in jails and other lockup environments for suspects and convicted criminals. Qualifications for the job vary with specific agencies, but an applicant must be eighteen years old, have a high school diploma or equivalent, and be a U.S. citizen with no felony convictions. In some cases, previous law enforcement or military experience can take the place of formal education. Furthermore, you will need to meet standards of physical strength, general health, and emotional stability, since you will sometimes be dealing with hostile persons.

If you meet the minimum requirements for becoming a photographer, correctional officer, or other support position, you will probably need only a relatively small amount of training before you can start your job. But, if you are on the road to being a sworn officer, it's a longer path to success. The application tests are just the beginning. You're now ready for a much greater test: being a **cadet** at a law enforcement academy.

AT THE ACADEMY

AT THE POLICE ACADEMY, WHERE FUTURE OFFICERS learn and practice the nuts and bolts of law enforcement, you will be tested far beyond the minimum requirements for making it through the application process. Your time in the police academy will also tell you if you are cut out for the job.

The competition is stiff. Thousands apply to academies across the country each year, and only a small percentage of the applicants are accepted. Even some of those who are accepted won't complete the course. Michigan State Trooper Shelley Izzard recalls, "My class started with about 120 [or] 125 people, and we graduated just under ninety people. . . . At the academy they told us that for every one hundred troopers that are sitting there, there are like 2,000 to 3,000 people who applied for those seats."

It is a sure bet that each of those troopers has made a serious commitment to making a difference. Washington State Patrol

Students at police academies learn both inside and outside the classroom. At this training session, an officer shows the proper way to subdue a suspect.

Sergeant Gundermann adds, "Every person who applies for a job in a law enforcement agency, somewhere in their interview they're going to be asked, 'Why do you want to be a trooper?' And 95 percent of them are going to say, 'I like to help people.'"

TWO TYPES OF TRAINING

Academies are typically associated with local or regional law enforcement agencies. The specific ways in which these academies are organized differ. Some are associated with universities. Many agencies operate their own academies. Others share facilities. In Washington State, for instance, all city, county, and state trainees attend one of two academies that the state operates. The trainees gain a solid knowledge base that is later "customized" by the specific agency they go to work for.

Some agencies are organized so that they hire future officers, send them to an academy, and guarantee a job when they graduate. The Washington State Patrol is typical of these agencies. Sergeant Gundermann, the WSP trooper, spells it out:

> Every trooper is hired as a cadet. From the time they're hired as a cadet, they're being evaluated. They initially receive about six weeks of basic training at our academy [but that] is just the basics.
>
> They're not troopers yet. They're given a limited commission [have standing as officers] and then they go out and provide security at ferry terminals, or the governor's mansion, and in a variety of other capacities.

Not all agencies are structured this way. Instead, some hire people who have graduated from schools called open-enrollment academies. If you graduate from an open academy, you'll then be applying for a job anywhere there is an opening. Generally speaking, graduates from these academies are headed for jobs at smaller agencies.

Of the two types of training facility, the agency-run kind is almost always preferable. Officer McCoy of the Houston PD comments, "A lot of smaller cities, they require you to pay for your own academy training. . . . These smaller cities don't have the money or the resources to send you to their own academy. But in bigger cities, once you're in the academy you're actually an employee."

THE MAKING OF A STATE TROOPER

Shelley Izzard's thoughtful description of her journey toward becoming a trooper in the Michigan State Police offers a useful perspective.

In college I thought my career would be elsewhere, but I struggled—I couldn't figure out how to help people the way I wanted to help people. I'd always been around police—my father was a magistrate, my godfather is a state trooper, my grandfather was the chief of police for a while, but I didn't really want to go that way.

But then I talked to a trooper and listened to how he could help people, and every day I thought about that, so I just changed my entire life and went this way and it's been great.

My advice is, don't wait. If you want to [go to the academy], do it right away. I waited, and I shouldn't have. For one thing, going through the academy at twenty-one as opposed to thirty-one—there are some significant differences!

I was training with twenty or twenty-one-year-olds, and I'm only 5'5," [so] some of those guys were a lot bigger. But I took that extra step every single day. That's the best advice I can give: When you think you've taken your last step, take one more. It's harder to recover from physical stress and strain when you're older. So the sooner you get in, the sooner you can get out and do what you want to and help the people who need you.

CODES OF DRESS AND CONDUCT

Many academies are residential (that is, students live on the facility's campus), although in some academies students are free to return home on weekends if they are close enough. The length of the training period that cadets will experience during this period differs according to the standards of individual academies, but the range is usually four to six months. Class sizes also vary, from about fifty students to more than two hundred for larger academies.

The physical facilities are typically set on large campuses, perhaps some distance from urban centers. For example, the Massachusetts State Police Academy encompasses 780 acres in a rural part of the state. This large campus includes buildings for classrooms, a dining hall, a firearms range, dormitories, a gymnasium, and an area where students take part in training drills that simulate real situations.

Academies are often referred to as "paramilitary organizations." That is, they are similar to the training facilities of the various branches of the military. As a result, they are run along the lines of boot camps, where discipline is tight and instructors and superiors have absolute authority over cadets.

This strict environment, where someone tells you what to do and you must do it without asking why, is not easy for many recruits to get used to. Nonetheless, it is a necessary part of the program, and most instructors and graduates will say that the result is worth the effort. Houston PD Officer McCoy comments:

In the academy you're trying to make it through, you're being drilled and you're being yelled at, doing pushups, and learning how to shoot and how to drive and make life-saving decisions. And [there are] spelling tests every day!

When you get through you really feel like you've accomplished something. The badge felt so light to me—I expected it to be this big, heavy-duty thing. I'd worked so hard to get it on my shirt. Still, it was a proud moment to put the uniform on after putting up with all that.

One aspect of the academy's paramilitary structure is that rules are thoroughly and carefully enforced. For example, administrators typically ban all alcohol, cigarettes, and drugs from the academy campus. Cadets must keep their dorm rooms extremely clean and neat, and this orderliness is subject to random spot checks. Attendance is mandatory for all classes and assemblies—in fact, in some cases no cadet can leave the facility, even for weekend breaks or for medical treatment, except by prior arrangement and for a good reason.

Most academies also resemble military units in their adherence to strict dress codes. For instance, the Massachusetts State Police Academy requires students to dress in uniform or business attire during regular hours. "Business attire" is defined as jackets and ties for men and suits for women. Jeans are not allowed at the Massachusetts facility except in certain training situations.

Training academies are structured a lot like boot camp. At the State Police Academy in Charlottesville, Virginia, trainees stand at attention, in their uniforms, for room inspection. The inspector uses a ruler to make sure the beds are made according to academy regulations.

Similar rules about personal appearance are in place at most other academies. For instance, at the New York State Police Academy, female recruits cannot use hair ornaments, ribbons, or earrings. Not even the use of cosmetics is allowed. Men must wear their hair short, and facial hair is prohibited.

Proper behavior, both on campus and off, is another strictly enforced aspect of life at the academy. Cadets are expected to remain calm, polite, and respectful at all times. Developing good habits in this area prepares the cadets to become professional officers in the field, where they will be dealing with the public. Breaking this rule—getting into a fight while off-campus, for instance—usually means discipline or, in extreme cases, dismissal from the program.

INSIDE AND OUTSIDE THE CLASSROOM

A typical day at a police academy begins at daybreak with roll call, and ends with lights-out at 10 p.m. In between, students participate in a variety of activities both inside and outside the classroom.

Much of the day is taken up with classroom work. To help them in their studies, recruits are generally provided with laptop computers and access to the academy's library. Typical classroom topics covered during this period include:

- Arrest and booking procedures
- Communications
- Community relations
- Crime scene investigations
- Cultural sensitivity training
- Defensive driving
- Domestic violence
- Elements of the law
  (such as general knowledge of regulations
  concerning search and seizure, evidence,
  and arrest policies)
- Ethics
- First aid
- Hate crimes
- Investigation techniques
- Leadership
- Missing persons
- Sexual harassment issues
- Team building

- Techniques and procedures for handling crimes in progress
- Traffic control and investigation
- Water safety

Not all of a cadet's training is in the classroom. Students also receive expert education and ample practice in such areas as pursuit on foot, surveillance, and defensive driving. They also take part in frequent practices that simulate real-life situations. Officer Elias of the Seattle Police Department recalls his academy days:

> At first there was a lot of classroom learning, but as you got further along there was a lot of practicing with scenarios, like role-playing confrontations or interviews where one guy would be the good guy, one the bad guy.
>
> [For these practices] we'd utilize what buildings were on the academy grounds. Some were outside on a sidewalk, and there was one building that had several mock rooms, like a bar or a bedroom, maybe four or five little rooms like that.

OUTSIDE THE CLASSROOM

An important part of academy training that takes place outside the classroom as well as in it concerns the proper use of force, both nonlethal and deadly. In formal classes, cadets learn about regulations concerning the proper use of such equipment as batons, pepper spray, and firearms. They learn that officers are authorized to use deadly force only in very specific situations—typically, when there is reasonable belief that the officer or someone else is in immediate danger of death or serious injury. Students learn that before deadly force is used, they must give multiple verbal warnings if at all possible.

San Antonio police officer Joseph Combs (*center*) reacts after being shocked by a taser during a demonstration of its proper use at a police academy training session.

Outside the classroom, they receive training and practice in the actual use of the weapons they will be carrying on the job. Training in all forms of firearms is stringent for the obvious reasons, and cadets must maintain extremely high marks in order to remain in the academy. Reaching a 90 percent accuracy rate with each category of firearms, including handguns and shotguns, is a typical requirement. Improper use of firearms is generally grounds for instant dismissal.

Also consistently emphasized outside the classroom is physical training. A typical day for you as a cadet will include a strenuous regimen of exercises for strength and conditioning. The intensity of these workouts increases gradually over the months you spend at the academy. For example, you might start out with a daily run of 1.5 miles (2.4 km), maintaining an 8-minute pace, and gradually increasing the distance to 5 miles (8 km) a day.

Cadets are tested several times throughout their training period to make sure they are maintaining their running skills and other forms of physical training. This exhausting schedule does not let up, but there is a reason and a purpose behind it. Michigan trooper Izzard recalls the windup of her months at the academy:

> Our graduation run was a 10-mile run (16 km) that we did as a class. And one morning we did 301 push-ups. 301 pushups! And if you were struggling and hit the deck you got right back up and kept going.
>
> That same day we had to qualify for a shotgun, and then we had to box with three people. They try to match you up with somebody equal in stature, but it's mixed men and women, and then they'll pair you up with somebody that could probably clean your clock. That was a pretty brutal day. My arms were dragging on the ground!
>
> [But] there's a lesson in there—to know what it's like to take a punch, and that you do not go down. You never, ever give up.

GRADUATING FROM THE ACADEMY

Life at the academy can be—and often is—highly competitive. Nonetheless, graduates frequently help each other out, and they typically form close and long-lasting friendships with each other. Officer Williamson of the Orlando PD recalls:

Training is hard, so graduation from the training academy is especially sweet. Here, police officers toss their white gloves in the air after graduating from the New York City Police Academy.

I went through with a group of about twenty who are still with the Orlando Police Department, and we're very good friends. Even with those of us who went to other agencies, you have that bond.

You really grow up together during those five months and really pull for each other, so if somebody was really good at something they'd help other people get through that part, and when you were weaker others could help you. So I think we're forever bonded by that experience.

When the months of hard work finally end, cadets are the honored guests at a proud and solemn moment—graduation.

A high point of this ceremony comes when the newly minted officers swear an oath of office—a promise that they will perform the duties and uphold the responsibilities of their jobs.

After taking the oath, you will be a sworn officer. Academies typically have their own specific oaths of office, but many use variations on the words used by the International Association of Chiefs of Police:

> On my honor, I will never betray my badge, my integrity, my character or public trust. I will always have the courage to hold myself and others accountable for our actions. I will always uphold the laws, my community and the agency I serve.

SUPPORT POSITIONS

A support position almost always requires less stringent training than a position as a sworn officer. Typically, you might receive a minimal amount of training under the guidance of a superior before you start work on your own. However, some support jobs require more thorough training.

For example, a forensics expert or dispatcher might need months of intensive instruction and on-the-job experience under the direction of a seasoned employee. Jobs like these generally require ongoing training and seminars. Leslie Lugo, the dispatcher in Dutchess County, New York, comments:

> I didn't have any special training before, but they have sent me to a lot of training since, which was wonderful.

[I have been trained to handle] hostage negotiation, domestic violence, and suicidal subjects.

It's great to get that kind of training, because a lot of times you get routine calls and you become kind of numb to them. So it's good to continuously have training to remind you that every call could be a potentially serious incident.

Another example of the kind of preparation required for a support job is provided by the typical training a correctional officer receives. People being trained for this position will first learn the overall regulations for the particular facility they will be working in. The training will include becoming familiar and comfortable with **custodial** and security procedures and policies.

Some correctional facilities require employees to have self-defense training and firearms certification. Joining a specialized team within a facility, such as a tactical response team, might also require training in advanced topics such as emergency management and forced-entry techniques, the proper handling of hazardous chemicals, and the latest means of dealing with hostage situations.

No matter what kind of job you are aiming for, and no matter how strenuous the training is, the general consensus among seasoned law enforcement professionals is that it is well worth the effort. Your reward for all that work? The start of a new career.

THREE

THE BIG PICTURE: HOW LAW ENFORCEMENT AGENCIES ARE ORGANIZED

WHETHER YOU ARE A BRAND NEW SWORN OFFICER or employed as a member of a law enforcement agency's support staff, you will be part of that agency's comprehensive overall structure. The way in which this structure works will determine, to a degree, what your experience will be like.

Often, it makes sense for city, county, and state agencies to organize themselves differently. After all, each level of law enforcement has specific duties and geographic areas to cover. While a city police department is responsible for a relatively small, densely populated, and concentrated area, a sheriff's office and a state patrol will cover much larger regions, often with extreme variations in geography (as found in states with large wilderness regions) and extreme variations in population density.

Agencies are organized differently depending on whether they are at the city, county, or state level. In densely populated cities like New York, you'll find police stations in heavily trafficked areas such as Times Square.

In any case, and in many ways, any one agency's organization will have much in common with every other agency at the same level. For example, in some ways all agencies will be structured to resemble the chain of command in a military organization, from the top commanders on down to the troops—the ones with their feet on the ground.

In other (and closely related) ways, your law enforcement agency's structure will resemble that of a typical office or company. In such cases, a president or director is at the top and the structure descends to the bottom ranks—people whose responsibilities are in places such as the company mailroom or motor pool.

If such a system is well structured and its positions filled by competent employees, the organization will operate smoothly and efficiently. A well-run organization will also provide its employees with ample opportunity to advance or change jobs. For example, a records clerk may become a dispatcher or office manager, which would be a step up in prestige, responsibilities, and pay. Similarly, an entry-level sworn officer can ascend the ranks to become a sergeant, senior officer, or member of top management, with corresponding steps up in pay and duties.

The organization of different agencies is certainly something you will want to consider as you explore a career in law enforcement. So is the relative size of a given agency. Interestingly, because of factors such as the specific duties involved, the size of a law enforcement agency is not always tied to the size of the geographic area it covers.

For example, in early 2011 the Chicago Police Department had more than 15,500 sworn officers and support personnel. Meanwhile, the sheriff's department for Cook County, the county around Chicago, had about 7,000—and the Illinois State Police had about 3,000 men and women to fulfill its task of enforcing the law on Illinois's highways.

HOW CITY POLICE DEPARTMENTS ARE ORGANIZED

The law enforcement agency you join probably will fall into one of several broad patterns of overall organization. One common pattern is to divide the agency geographically and physically. For example, a police department typically divides its city into sections called precincts—East Precinct, North Precinct, and so on.

Each of these precincts has a police station that serves as that district's central headquarters. The precincts are then divided into smaller areas called sectors, and sectors are divided into still smaller portions called beats. Beats are the areas patrolled by individual officers.

Another common and logical way to view an agency's organization is to identify employees as belonging to one of two general groups: one of sworn officers, the other of support personnel. A good example is the police department in Iowa City, Iowa. This agency's employees work either in field operations (the sworn officers) or administrative services (the support personnel).

The largest component of Iowa City's Field Operations Division (and of most agencies) consists of police who are "on the street" (patrol officers and detectives) and in management (supervisors and administrators, who are usually officers promoted from lower ranks). In Iowa City, technical positions such as photographers and forensic specialists are part of the Field Operations Division. However, in some cities these roles are filled by nonsworn support employees or are outsourced elsewhere in the community.

As is typical in other parts of the country, Iowa City's field officers work in three shifts, called watches. Each watch is supervised by three managers (that is, officers who have been promoted from the field). This way of splitting up responsibilities between three shifts ensures that officers are on duty twenty-four hours a day and seven days a week. Meanwhile,

In addition to law enforcement agents, every police department requires support staff.

many support staff employees, such as dispatchers and fingerprint analysts, also work different shifts to make sure that information is received and handled in a timely manner.

The other portion of the Iowa City force, like its counterparts across the country, is its Administrative Services Division. (The sections and responsibilities of a city police agency's administrative departments, which take care of such duties as office management, are generally mirrored in county and state agencies as well.)

Like their counterparts in other law enforcement agencies, Iowa City's support group of civilian (nonsworn) employees provides a variety of services for field operations. The jobs in the support network of a police force are similar in any given law enforcement agency, although they might exist under different names.

HOW LAW ENFORCEMENT AGENCIES ARE ORGANIZED

LEVELS OF RESPONSIBILITY

The organizational aspects of policing are fairly standard for agencies in different parts of the country. However, the specifics vary greatly depending on specific circumstances. For example, a major city like Detroit and a small town in Nevada have very different needs in law enforcement, and the specific needs will determine the size of a given agency. A small-town agency may have half a dozen officers and a dozen—or even fewer—support staffers. An agency in a big city, meanwhile, will have thousands of officers, upper management, and support staff.

Individuals at given levels have different primary duties. For example, within a field department, patrol officers ("beat cops") are responsible for monitoring certain sectors of their precincts and responding to calls from the public. Detectives, meanwhile, are higher on the chain of command and are in charge of follow-up investigations, usually of serious crimes such as homicide, domestic abuse, and robbery.

The separation of jobs within an agency's field operations is fluid, however, and can change as circumstances change. Specialized teams are often organized by drawing personnel from various levels of authority. For example, a squad devoted to robbery might be composed of individuals from higher ranks of management, detectives and field officers, as well as support personnel such as weapons technicians and crime scene analysts. These teams might be permanent, or they might be assembled to tackle a single task, such as investigating a series of break-ins.

COMMUNITIES, DOGS, AND DETECTIVES

In addition to being organized by rank, geographical boundaries, and responsibilities, law enforcement agencies can be organized by creating separate groups that focus on specialized tasks. For example, in many cities, patrol officers are assigned to community police teams (CPTs).

In pairs or individually, CPT officers stay within a small area, covering perhaps only a few neighborhoods and focusing on long-term problems. For example, they might concentrate on gang activity by patrolling a single area regularly. At the same time, CPTs get to know the people who live in their neighborhoods and understand their concerns, and vice versa. The Seattle Police Department website notes, "While patrol officers assigned to a certain beat and sector are usually very familiar with the area they patrol, CPT Officers go one step further."

Another example of a specialized unit is a K-9 corps—a team that uses specially trained dogs. Typically, a K-9 corps features specialists of two kinds: drug dogs, which sniff out illegal drugs, and patrol dogs, which track wanted suspects on the run or missing persons.

An unusual aspect of K-9 teams is that officers typically do not rotate out after a few years, as is often the case in other positions. Instead, they remain for the length of their dogs' on-duty lives, usually five or six years. For the duration of their active service, dogs live at the homes of their human partners, a practice that serves to maintain especially close bonds.

Meanwhile, a familiar type of specialized team is that of detectives—the men and women who investigate and solve crimes. Being a detective requires skill, intelligence, and persistence, so making the cut is difficult. Detectives are usually sergeants, and some elite units will not consider an applicant with less than ten years of patrol experience.

There are many specific types of work. For example, narcotics detectives focus on drug trafficking and use. Homicide detectives investigate murders. Others tackle categories including physical or sexual abuse, missing persons, unidentified bodies, identity theft, organized crime, major robberies, fraud, and gang-related activity.

One highly specialized type of detective work focuses on the forensic analysis of major traffic accidents. The purpose is to reconstruct exactly what happened and why. For example, the Major Accident Response and Reconstruction (MARR) Unit of the King County (Washington) Sheriff's Office uses traditional detective work as well as cutting-edge tools and techniques, such as 3-D computer imaging and specialized photography.

Above: K-9 units have become essential to many law enforcement agencies in the United States.

THE CHAIN OF COMMAND

The specific responsibilities and titles of a given position within a field division will vary from agency to agency. Typically, however, they follow a military-style chain of command. In the case of sworn officers, these titles are usually borrowed from military organizations.

At the top of an agency, with the ultimate responsibility for managing both officers and support personnel, is a police chief. He or she is responsible for managing the entire operation. As a rule, officers in these high positions report directly to the appropriate top government official. In the case of a city police chief, this is the mayor.

Below the top authority in the agency, the rest of the chain of command descends down through many more levels. In descending order, a typical overall chain of command might look like this:

- Chief of Police
- Deputy Chief
- Assistant Chief
- Inspector
- Deputy Inspector
- Major
- Captain
- Lieutenant
- Sergeant
- Detective
- Patrol officers
- Support personnel

Usually, all levels of a law enforcement agency's field operations are made up of sworn officers. However, there are exceptions. For example, both New York City and Boston have police departments headed by civilians who are appointed by the mayor. These administrators are called police commissioners. Below the commissioners are a number of deputy commissioners and other members of top management.

In theory, the military-style chain of command within a law enforcement agency allows information and orders to flow smoothly, from the head of the organization to its most junior member. At the same time, this chain theoretically works in reverse, allowing information, ideas, suggestions, or comments to flow upward from junior members of the force to higher levels.

Within the overall structure of a typical agency's field operations are several sublevels. For example, detectives can be junior or senior detectives (also called detectives first-class). Another example is found in the New York City Police Department, which classifies its detectives as detective-investigators and detective-specialists. Generally, detective-investigators do just that—they investigate serious crimes such as murder, rape, or major fraud. Detective-specialists, meanwhile, focus on a special skill: some are sharpshooters; some are bomb technicians; others are helicopter instructors. As the title suggests, they have the same rank as detective-investigators.

The various departments within support sections are similarly subdivided. Generally, they are organized in a way much like that of a typical office or company. For example, a person whose duties are like those of an office manager would be responsible for overseeing dispatchers and the other employees within that office. As is true in manufacturing or commerce, entry-level positions, in both field operations and support operations, are at the bottom of the seniority ladder.

HOW COUNTY LAW ENFORCEMENT AGENCIES ARE ORGANIZED

Generally speaking, county sheriff's offices are organized in similar ways to city police departments. They have military-style chains of command and are divided into groups for both generalized and specific duties.

A representative example of how a sheriff's office is organized is that of King County, Washington, the county around Seattle. King County is the most heavily populated in the state, and its sheriff's force is the largest in the state. It has more than 1,000 employees, including sworn deputies and support staff. (Contrast this with the sheriff's department in rural Yakima County, in south central Washington, which has about 90 employees in total.)

The King County Sheriff's Office has five general sections: the Office of the Sheriff and four divisions under it. Each of the sections has a particular set of goals and responsibilities.

The Office of the Sheriff is the agency's main administrative department. In addition to the sheriff, the Office of the Sheriff includes a number of aides and support staff; there is a legal section and a media relations officer, who serves as a link between the department and news media. Another important part of the Office of the Sheriff is its Internal Investigations Unit. This section is in charge of examining possible misconduct within the agency itself.

The Criminal Investigations Division, one of the four main departments in King County's Office of the Sheriff, is further subdivided into three groups: the Major Crimes Section, the Special Investigations Section, and the Regional Criminal Intelligence Group. The duties of these teams include investigating and serving warrants for such major crimes as homicide, domestic violence, computer fraud, forgery, and sexual assault.

The second main department under the Office of the Sheriff is the Field Operations Division. These men and women handle the day-to-day duties that are not covered by the Criminal Investigations Division. Within Field Operations are teams made up of patrol deputies, crime prevention units, and reserve deputies. Separation of the Field Operations Division into four geographic precincts makes it easier for the Sheriff's Office to respond quickly to a variety of situations anywhere in the county.

The third main department is the Special Operations Division. This group is responsible for specialized teams that provide a variety of services in support of other divisions. Among these are such tasks as K-9 deployment, air and water support, bomb and hazardous materials handling, traffic enforcement, search and rescue, hostage negotiation, and homeland security procedures. The Special Operations Division also coordinates the "loan" of sheriff's deputies and other personnel, when requested, to a variety of other agencies when, for example, such assistance is requested by the county's transportation system or its ports.

The fourth main department within the King County Sheriff's Office, the Technical Services Division, is roughly equivalent to the administrative departments in other law enforcement agencies. Its responsibilities include receiving emergency calls and dispatching officers, information technology development and maintenance, photography, and forensic work. In addition, Technical Services provides administrative support to the other teams and groups within the sheriff's agency, such as coordinating communication and cooperation with the county's residents and citizen groups.

"ONE RIOT, ONE RANGER"

Of all the law enforcement agencies across the United States, one famous group deserves special mention: the Texas Rangers. Organized in 1823, the Rangers are the nation's oldest state-level team of officers.

Nearly two hundred years ago, these legendary agents were integral to the legends of the Old West's freewheeling frontier. Today, the Rangers are an important part of Texas's law enforcement community. There are only about 150 Rangers to police the vast territory of Texas which covers 268,820 square miles (696,240 km). This means that each officer in this elite agency has jurisdiction over at least two or three large counties.

The Rangers are a separate agency from the Texas State Troopers although their duties can overlap somewhat. In practice, Texas State Troopers primarily focus on highway patrol and some criminal investigation, while Rangers focus on the investigation of major crimes.

Texas Rangers have a reputation for being among the toughest and most self-reliant officers in the nation. As a former captain in the agency puts it, "A Ranger is an officer who is able to handle any given situation without definite instructions from his commanding officer or higher authority."

This reputation for self-reliance and toughness has given rise to a well-known motto: One riot, one Ranger.

HOW STATE LAW ENFORCEMENT AGENCIES ARE ORGANIZED

Each of the fifty states has its own law enforcement agency, in addition to city police and county sheriffs. The officers who work at the third level go by a variety of official titles. Some are called state police, while others are referred to as state troopers, state patrol, or highway patrol. Broadly speaking, these terms are interchangeable.

The exact duties and areas of authority of these agencies vary somewhat from state to state. For example, in several states, such as California, Illinois, and Florida, troopers have **jurisdiction**, primarily concerning safety measures and criminal activity along state roads, highways, and other property, such as state parks. They are responsible for writing speeding tickets, enforcing laws concerning fire safety on state property, and coordinating rescue and cleanup activity at the scene of traffic accidents.

In sparsely populated states, where city and county law enforcement agencies are typically small or even nonexistent, state agencies often have much broader powers. This is especially true in rural or wilderness areas that do not come under another agency's authority. For example, a state patrol's scope might include acting as the law enforcement agency for a community that is too small to have its own police force.

State trooper agencies are organized in ways that are generally similar to city and county agencies. However, there are some differences in how they are structured. For instance, the Division of Alaska State Troopers has four main bureaus: the Bureau of Highway Patrol, the Bureau of Investigation, the Bureau of Alcohol and Drug Enforcement, and the Bureau of Judicial Services (which transports prisoners and provides security for the state's courts and government officials). These are further subdivided into more specialized teams. For instance, the Alaska Bureau of Investigation incorporates the Major Crimes Unit, the Computer and Financial Crimes Unit, and the Missing Persons Unit.

The organization of the law enforcement agency you join may differ a bit from those of other agencies. This is true whether you become a sworn officer or a member of the agency's support staff. In any case, being on the job will be a new and interesting experience.

ON THE JOB

NO TWO JOBS IN LAW ENFORCEMENT ARE THE same. Some support staff positions, such as records keeping or administrative duties, have relatively steady schedules and duties. Other support positions are more unpredictable. For example, a dispatcher has to handle several things at once when an emergency strikes or a major crime is discovered. A photographer or forensics expert will be dealing with new situations in the field or lab every day.

In many law enforcement jobs, you will be in daily contact with people—real people with real problems. Some work situations are unpredictable and volatile, especially for officers in the field. Those situations, however, are relatively rare. In a typical breakdown of duties, a police officer, deputy sheriff, or state trooper might find that 25 percent of his or her time is spent on paperwork, such as filling out accident reports; 70 percent on routine patrol and answering everyday calls; and only 5 percent on pursuits or other high-risk activities.

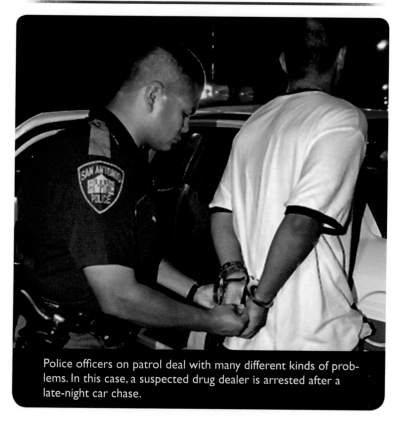

Police officers on patrol deal with many different kinds of problems. In this case, a suspected drug dealer is arrested after a late-night car chase.

BEING A ROOKIE

In many cases, if you are hired as a support employee, you will be up to speed quickly, without much training needed. However, the work environment is different for officers. As a sworn officer, your first years will be as a **rookie**, and you will have a lot to learn on the job regardless of whether you work at a city, county, or state agency.

As a rookie officer, you will be assigned to a shift on patrol. It's an important job—beat cops (and their equivalents in sheriff and state patrol agencies) may have the greatest day-to-day impact on their community of anyone on the force. They get to know the people on their beats, are often the first to respond to crimes or crisis situations, and sometimes prevent crime just by their presence.

As a new officer, you will go through a probationary period, the length of which varies from agency to agency. You'll be supervised by at least one senior officer to "customize" the basic education you got at the academy. Officer Elias of the Seattle PD recalls of his experience,

> After the academy [you] have a phase where you go with three experienced officers for a month each, and they teach you the ropes. They teach you stuff specific to your department: this is how we do building searches, this is how we do paperwork.

Following your probationary period, you will be automatically promoted, with more responsibilities and freedom to work on your own. At this point you usually can ask for certain assignments—for example, a precinct close to home and a watch that best suits you.

WHAT OFFICERS DO

As is true of many other aspects of work in law enforcement, the daily responsibilities of officers vary widely. To take an obvious example, a police officer working an inner city beat will have experiences very different from those of a state trooper on a rural highway.

Nonetheless, some things tend to be similar for patrol officers in city, county, and state organizations, and many of the tasks are the same. These typical duties include the following:

- Assisting drivers in trouble and monitoring traffic safety
- Conducting initial interviews of suspects and witnesses
- Giving expert or eyewitness testimony in court
- Making arrests, booking suspects, and collecting evidence
- Monitoring suspicious activity
- Preparing daily reports
- Recovering stolen property
- Responding at the scene of a crime or accident
- Responding to citizens' and visitors' questions
- Visiting local businesses and neighborhood watch meetings to establish relationships

Many patrol officers choose to keep doing the same job for years. They like the feeling of belonging that comes with staying on the same beat and getting to know the individuals they serve. Another reason some officers choose to keep a familiar beat is that they can stay on patrol but also join special units. For example, when emergency situations arise, a trooper can be temporarily assigned to such groups as a hostage negotiation team.

On the other hand, officers can also request a change after three or four years. A transfer might mean joining a specialized division, such as a detective unit or other team. Among the most common of these specialized positions are the following:

- Bomb and hazardous waste disposal
- Community relations
- Crime scene investigation
- Crisis negotiation
- Diver

- Fire/Arson investigation
- K-9 Corps (handler on a drug-sniffing dog team)
- School resource officer
- Search and rescue

Moving on to one of these positions by no means requires you to stay there. In fact, much of the appeal of police work is the ability to participate in many groups over the years. Sergeant Gundermann of the Washington State Patrol comments, "If you're assigned to [a region or position] right out of the academy you can stay there for twenty-five years . . . if you want to. [But] you can move around a lot. That makes it pretty fun."

Some agencies like to rotate officers into different squads every few years. This gives the officers education and experience in a range of police work. Sergeant Gundermann adds that being in a new situation helps relieve some of the pressure of being on patrol all the time. He states, "You kind of get your sanity back and get reenergized to get back on the road. Because working the road is very demanding. . . . You need to break it up a little bit."

SUPPORT POSITIONS

As with patrol work, the daily responsibilities of support staff vary considerably. Some support positions can be as fast moving and stressful as patrol work. For example, one of the most important jobs in any law enforcement agency is that of a dispatcher.

A dispatcher's daily work is busy, complex, and demanding. He or she receives emergency calls, and then alerts the

A DAY IN THE LIFE OF A CITY PATROL OFFICER

No matter where they work, law enforcement officers consistently describe their jobs by saying that no day is exactly like another. However, there are some things that are typical or routine events. Officer Adam Elias of the Seattle Police Department describes such a day:

> I have Third Watch, which in Seattle is 7:30 at night till 4:30 in the morning. Our squad has about twelve people. I'll usually get into the precinct a little after seven, and we have a locker room so I can get changed into my uniform with my [equipment] belt and [bulletproof] vest and everything.
>
> And then we have roll call, where you and your squad sit down with the sergeants in a room and they go over anything that happens the night before or that day, and other information, like if there's a particular burglar they're looking for, and they'll assign who's working where.
>
> [Then] we head out. Seattle has pool cars, which means we don't have our own vehicles, so you have to go out and check out a vehicle, and put all your assorted gear in the car. We have what we call our kit, which has all the paperwork you might need, accident reports, tickets. A lot of the stuff we do is on computer now but we also still have a lot on paper. And we have our riot helmets and riot batons and gas masks with us everywhere we go, in case something happens.
>
> Once we get in our cars we log on with our computers so that they know where we are and that we're available. If there are no calls waiting we just go out on patrol, we have our own specific areas where we go, and we'll just drive around and look for things that might be not right.

Above: Computers have become an essential part of law enforcement, even for officers on the beat.

appropriate officers so that they can respond quickly. Dispatchers are also sometimes called on to coordinate search and rescue missions or other jobs that require close monitoring of many different aspects of a situation. There are few dull moments in a dispatcher's job; depending on the size of the force and the area covered, a law enforcement agency might receive and respond to tens of thousands of phone calls a year.

Being a dispatcher requires the ability to handle emergency situations efficiently, calmly, swiftly, and completely. Failure to act intelligently and coolly can mean the difference between life and death, for civilians as well as officers. Often, officers responding to potentially dangerous situations know little about what has happened. In such cases, they rely on dispatchers to provide needed information.

The dispatcher's job requires good skills in communication (to clearly understand and convey information) and specialized areas (to handle the monitoring technology itself and keep officers informed). Also, however, it requires good "people skills." Leslie Lugo, the dispatcher in Dutchess County, New York, comments,

> I sometimes feel like I'm a therapist, or a referee. Like if it's husband-wife issues and they're screaming at each other, you try to calm the situation down.
>
> It can be very stressful, but I find it rewarding. Not all the time, but a majority of the time, you're able to help people and guide them and find solutions to whatever issues they may be having. My main goal is always to try and make the situation calm for the officer that is responding.

DISPATCHERS: THE EYES AND EARS OF LAW ENFORCEMENT

Dispatchers (also called telecommunicators) are responsible for taking calls from the public or officers, then coordinating the proper response. Leslie Lugo, a dispatcher for the Dutchess County (New York) Sheriff's Office, has this to say about her job:

I am the eyes and ears of the officer, basically. I answer all calls that come into our department and I dispatch officers to all types of calls. The number of calls varies from day to day. I'd have to say an average eight-hour day would be forty-five to fifty calls.

You have to be a multitasker. You keep the person on the phone while you're in communication with the officer. A lot of it is touch-screen, so you're able to stay on the phone and with your other hand get the officer on the radio and give them the information about the incident.

And a lot of times we're able to communicate with the officers through chat [via the Internet], so I can send them stuff [that way] if it's not information that I want going over the air or if I don't want to let the person know I'm calling the officer. But most of the time I do tell [the officers] over the radio system, and they and any additional backup units can know what's going on.

I deal with domestic incident calls, mother-son, father-daughter domestic disputes. I deal with extremely emotionally disturbed people, children calling requesting help because there are issues at home, elderly people, all kinds of people and all kinds of problems.

What I find rewarding is a lot of times being able to help—because when [people] call they are calling for help. Just being able to provide any type of assistance to them, like if you're talking to someone who is emotionally disturbed.

We don't have to, but it's good to get on a personal basis with the callers. A lot of times I have used personal experience to let them know that I understand what they may be feeling. Getting a rapport with them is always extremely important. You don't want them ever to hang up or get disconnected, because that's a very hard thing, losing a phone call when it's a serious incident.

INFORMATION TECHNOLOGY, TECHNICAL SUPPORT, FORENSICS SUPPORT, AND AIDES

Additional important members of the support staff of any law enforcement agency are its experts in information technology (IT) and other areas requiring technical support. These law enforcement staffers often have daily duties that go far beyond the installation and maintenance of the agency's computer networks and equipment such as surveillance gear. They are also frequently able to provide crucial, urgent help to officers who are involved in ongoing investigations.

For example, a computer specialist might become part of a team that is actively investigating crimes such as identity theft, financial fraud, hacking, or child pornography. An expert in surveillance, meanwhile, can be equally important to an investigation that calls for his or her skills in gathering and analyzing information from computers, cell phones, and other sources.

Meanwhile, forensic artists can provide similarly crucial support for investigative teams that have immediate need for it. Forensic artists create portraits of suspects based on eyewitness accounts. This kind of work typically has to be done quickly and accurately, so that investigations can move swiftly ahead.

Although speed isn't always possible, accuracy is also required on the part of forensic specialists who focus on the scientific side of inquiries into criminal activity. Their work often involves specialized testing of biological, chemical, and physical evidence such as the following:

Forensics is at the heart of many crime investigations. Here, an officer uses magnetic power brushes on the inside of a car window as he dusts for prints on a vehicle used in a homicide.

- Blood alcohol level testing
- Bullet and weapons identification
- DNA and blood analysis
- Drug identification
- Fingerprint identification
- Tire track identification
- Toxicology (poison identification)

Equally important work is done by other key members of a law enforcement agency's forensic support staff. These include evidence technicians, medical examiners, and coroners. Medical examiners are experts who collect and analyze medical evidence at the scene of a crime. Coroners specialize in autopsies—procedures that thoroughly examine bodies to determine the cause of death and to bring to light facts not knowable without dissection.

Some law enforcement agencies hire employees called support (or sheriff's) aides. Aides are typically hired by agencies that are not large enough to need full-time employees for specific jobs. As a result, aides must be good at handling many tasks at the same time, switching quickly from one to another, often on the same day. While these assignments generally are not dangerous, the work is fast moving and full of variety.

The position of aide in the Kern County (California) Sheriff's Office is a typical one. It involves such duties as recording civil and criminal complaints, delivering and tracking summonses, monitoring supplies and inventory, maintaining databases and files, securing evidence, and maintaining and coordinating vehicles and equipment. Other usual responsibilities for aides include fingerprinting and photographing inmates, receiving public complaints, tracking the collection of evidence, and maintaining order during visitation rights in jail facilities.

TRANSLATORS AND PHOTOGRAPHERS

In addition to the varied support jobs already mentioned, you can apply for many other positions within an agency. For example, city police departments typically need parking enforcers and personnel to handle nonemergency calls. And there are many other opportunities to work in specialized jobs.

One example is the position of translator. Police officers are always under stress on the job. Trying to communicate with someone who doesn't speak their language is very likely to worsen this stress. Having a translator on hand makes the officer's work easier, more effective, and sometimes, safer. The ability to communicate clearly and quickly can mean the difference between life and death.

Translators often work part-time or on-call (that is, as needed), although some large cities have full-time translators on staff. Sometimes you will do your job inside the office, translating documents or helping officers take statements or interrogate suspects. However, you will also frequently go out in the field with officers, working beside them to communicate with law-abiding citizens and suspects alike. Translators are further needed during court trials, to ensure that statements and instructions are clearly and fully understood.

Being a photographer is another crucial support position that, like translating, is performed indoors and out. Your daily work as a photographer will be varied. Sometimes it will involve fairly routine tasks such as cataloging photos or taking portraits of agency employees for licensing requirements. Sometimes you will be taking pictures of suspects and convicted criminals who are being processed in or out of the justice system, and at other times you will work in unusual or challenging situations, such as doing nighttime or aerial photography.

Furthermore, the work will also involve teaming with detectives to prepare evidence for court appearances or presentations to the media. And you will also be called on to record and analyze crime scenes. This field, called forensic photography, requires a considerable amount of highly specialized training. In any case, no matter what tasks you have as a photographer, the daily work will involve close attention to detail, strong organizational skills, and high technical expertise.

Doing this job well is not just a matter of technical abilities, however. An effective law enforcement photographer also must be sensitive. This is because, as with other jobs in law enforcement, you need a good understanding of how your work affects the victims of crimes, their families, and others. In other words, you need to be respectful in situations where your presence might otherwise be seen as offensive or inappropriate. A grieving family, for example, might resent your presence at a crime scene, so you need to act in a way that discreetly persuades them that what you do is necessary and for their good.

BOSTON MARATHON BOMBING

On April 15, 2013, organizers of the Boston marathon were ready for the race. Fifty-seven off-duty detailed personnel worked the marathon, in addition to the 267 on-duty men and women who normally work a day shift. There were also special teams positioned in the crowd and assigned to each Boston block of the 26.2-mile (42.1 km) marathon, which winds through eight cities and towns. They watched to make sure everyone progressed to the finish line, the obvious goal of all runners.

While there was no direct intelligence, the threat of a terrorist attack always exists. The team members were equipped with protective clothing and medical kits in the unlikely event that something would happen. When the first bomb exploded, panic ensued among runners and spectators alike. The first responders acted right away. In less than half an hour, the last victim was moved off the street to receive triage of some kind of medical treatment.

OTHER SUPPORT POSITIONS

The many other jobs that fall within the category of law enforcement support positions all have their own set of daily responsibilities. Some examples are found in the areas of property custody, records, community relations, and equipment maintenance.

The Property Custody Department is responsible for handling and storing pieces of evidence or property, returning items to their rightful owners, submitting evidence to crime labs for analysis, and destroying or auctioning unclaimed items that are no longer required as evidence. This position's duties run from the start to finish of a given case, since evidence must be carefully accounted for, cataloged, stored, and retrieved as requested all along the way.

Records units store documentation for law enforcement agencies. A police force's responses to calls for service, traffic accidents, criminal activity, parking violations, and other incidents all involve paperwork and documentation. The paperwork must be properly catalogued and safely stored, since officers may need to refer to it later. This will be your responsibility as a records specialist.

A specialist in community relations typically will have primary responsibility for creating and maintaining connections between your law enforcement agency and the community it serves. For example, you will work with government employees and citizen groups to organize such activities as school educational programs, neighborhood watches, and community meetings.

Equipment maintenance duties in law enforcement

agencies generally go to civilian employees who maintain the agency's vehicles, firearms, helicopters and other aircraft, and any other equipment that is needed on an everyday basis. Your role as an equipment maintenance specialist will be to make sure that all these vital tools are in good working order.

CORRECTIONAL OFFICERS

Correctional officers (sometimes called detention officers) are responsible for processing people in and out of jails, reformatories, or penitentiaries; maintaining order and security there; and in general watching over inmates who are awaiting trial or have been convicted of crimes. A small percentage of corrections officers work in for-profit businesses. However, most work in government facilities.

Good correctional officers are in high demand because the number of prisoners is enormous. As of 2011, local facilities across the country were processing a total of some 13 million people a year, and watching over nearly 800,000 offenders at any given time. State and federal prisons, meanwhile, account for another 1.6 million offenders at any given time. (Generally, offenders sentenced to a year or less are in county jails, while those serving longer sentences are housed in state or federal prisons and penitentiaries.)

Being a correctional officer in a jail or prison is, without question, a tough job. The duties include searching inmates and their cells for illegal items such as weapons or drugs, breaking up fights between inmates, and enforcing discipline. If you are a correctional officer, you will also regularly patrol and inspect your facility, checking for unsanitary conditions, security risks, fire hazards, or evidence of violations of rules. In addition, you will be responsible for inspecting mail and making sure that visitors do not bring in prohibited items. You will also be transporting or escorting prisoners within the facility or to and from outside places such as courtrooms and hospitals. You may be called on to aid in searches for escaped prisoners.

At every step, your duties will also include keeping a log documenting your activities and observances. Depending on specific facilities and situations, you may or may not be armed, but you will routinely have communications equipment, such as cell phones or radios, in case you encounter trouble. Again depending on specifics, you may be patrolling the facility in person, or keeping track of activity via closed-circuit television and computer tracking.

Another type of correctional officer is the bailiff. Bailiffs are law enforcement officers who are assigned to courtrooms. Your daily responsibilities as a bailiff will typically include keeping order in the court, helping judges with duties such as the handling of evidence, making sure that **sequestered** juries do not have contact with the outside, and providing messenger services for court documents.

Whether you are working as a correctional officer, in another support position, or as a sworn officer, you will have the personal satisfaction that comes from knowing that you are making your community better and safer. As with any other job, law enforcement agencies offer their employees a range of salaries and benefits.

SALARY AND BENEFITS

A CAREER IN A CITY, COUNTY, OR STATE LAW enforcement agency is a good bet in terms of salary and benefits. For one thing, the salaries and benefits for entry-level positions are typically much better than those in other fields.

Also, aiming for a career in law enforcement, either as a sworn officer or as a civilian employee, is an excellent way to boost your chances of getting and keeping a job. That is, your chances of finding a job are generally better, as are your chances of avoiding unemployment, than with other careers. There will always be a market for people who can deal effectively with criminals and provide good support for those in the field, because it is a grim fact that there will always be crime.

Not just anyone can do a good job of upholding the law, so law enforcement recruiting departments must pick the best-qualified and most capable employees—the ones who can do the job best. Of course, it is then important to keep those employees happy. In general, law enforcement agencies

Promotions and awards let police officers know that their hard work is appreciated. Many police departments, such as this one in Washington, D.C., hold annual award and promotion ceremonies.

offer attractive packages of salary and benefits to employees at all levels, including entry-level positions. These employees are unionized, and the unions negotiate favorable salaries and benefits for their members.

MOVING UP THE LADDER
FOR PATROL OFFICERS

If you are planning to be a sworn officer on a city, county, or state level, the type of academy you attend will often be an important factor in determining your future income. If you are hired by a law enforcement agency that sends its recruits to an academy, you will start drawing a salary on the first day of training. The agency will also pay many of your expenses during training, and it will guarantee you a job. When your training is complete and you officially become part of the force, you will receive an automatic pay raise.

However, if you attend an open-enrollment academy, you will have out-of-pocket expenses. You will have to pay for your academy fees and living expenses while on campus, and you won't start drawing a salary until an agency has hired you. Also, if you go an open-enrollment school, the chances are good that the positions available to you will be with small, less prestigious, or less challenging agencies.

No matter where you took your training, however, once you have worked as an officer on a force for a few years, you will be eligible for pay increases and promotion. Typically, eligibility for promotion comes up two to four years after hiring. Promotions then generally progress in set stages—in other words, you move up step by step, with each step bringing an increase in pay and responsibilities.

The speed at which you make this progress can vary greatly, depending on factors that include performance reviews ("report cards" indicating how well you are doing), as well as your level of education. For example, new recruits with college degrees are paid more than those with only high school degrees. If you choose to attend college at night, earning a degree while working, you will improve your chances of advancement to sergeant, the next step after patrol officer.

DIFFERENCES IN PAY

Overall, the salaries for beginning police officers and sheriff's deputies are typical of beginning salaries in comparable fields of employment. Nationwide, they average about $30,000. Individually, however, pay may vary widely from agency to agency.

IN THE SCHOOLS:
SCHOOL RESOURCE OFFICERS

Officer Jennifer Williamson of the Orlando (Florida) Police Department, has this to say about her duties as a School Resource Officer:

> A school officer is the first line of defense, [because] students need to get to know us and trust us. If they have a good officer in school, they can have a good relationship with the police when they're not in school.
>
> If we can really be there for [the students] and listen to them when they need us, that's going to [shape] their opinion of us [the police]. When I'm on the street with them in the future they might keep that trust. I'm in a school where a lot of people have a bad opinion of police, even though they may never [have] had any grounds for it, so I try to work hard to change that.
>
> I like my interactions with kids. I like trying to instill in kids that the real-life . . . decisions they make today in middle school can affect them in their future. It can affect whether you go to college, whether you get into the college you want to go to.
>
> A lot of the kids I deal with don't have family who are able to tell them you can do better, and that you can't be getting into trouble and expect that a college football team is going to want you to play for them, or whatever. [So I try] to impart a small part of my knowledge and personality when I interact with the kids.

Above: A police officer plays chess with students in an inner city junior high school to let them know that a police officer is someone who can be trusted rather than feared.

In many cases, police officers in large urban centers can expect to earn more than those in a small town or rural area. For example, in 2011, the Los Angeles Police Department's minimum entry-level salary for officers with high-school diplomas or GED equivalents was about $45,200.

The LAPD is also typical of agencies that adjust their pay scales for officers who have attended college. In 2011 a rookie LAPD officer could start at about $47,000 if he or she already had sixty or more college credits with an overall GPA of 2.0 or better. New officers with four-year college degrees, meanwhile, started their careers at nearly $49,000. Salaries were even higher for officers with previous experience in related work environments, such as the military.

Sometimes the pay is progressively less as cities or regions drop in population. However, this is not always the case. For instance, compare the pay range in Los Angeles to that of Minneapolis, Minnesota. The population of Minneapolis is about 377,000, while Los Angeles has about 4 million residents. However, in 2011 the base salary range for a new recruit in Minneapolis, depending on education and experience, was roughly $45,500 to $50,200. So, despite the difference in size, the pay range is roughly the same for both police forces.

Some small towns or cities pay significantly more than larger cities. For example, affluent cities have larger tax bases, so their residents pay more taxes. As a result, city budgets are larger and the cities can pay their employees more. A good example is Mercer Island, Washington, a wealthy suburb of Seattle. In 2011 Mercer Island (population 22,890) paid a starting patrol officer with a two-year college degree nearly $57,000.

COUNTY DEPUTY SHERIFFS
AND STATE TROOPERS

The factors affecting the salaries of county sheriff's deputies and state troopers vary, just like those of city police officers. In many cases, they reflect the size of the populations they serve. For example, in 2011 in Harris County, Texas (which surrounds Houston and has a population of about 4 million), the starting pay for deputy sheriffs was $40,643.

Another example is the sheriff's department in Wicomico County, Maryland (population about 95,000). The base salary there for new deputy sheriffs as of 2011 was about $39,300. In much smaller Dane County, Wisconsin (population about 50,000), the sheriff's office paid its first-year deputies slightly more—about $40,300.

Contrast these with Esmeralda County, Nevada, which has about 1,240 residents for the entire juris-diction. There, the salary for a rookie cop in 2011 was only about $29,500. Of course, lower pay in rural areas like Esmeralda County is generally offset by other factors, such as the lower cost of housing and other living expenses.

In some ways, the salaries for officers on the state level reflect factors similar to those that influence pay scales at other levels of law enforcement. The amounts vary somewhat, but overall salaries are in the same range as county and city agencies.

Salaries for state troopers are often tied to the size of the population they serve.

For example, the Ohio State Patrol paid about $44,500 to its troopers in early 2011, while its counterpart in Colorado paid about $50,000. (Interestingly, Ohio has over twice as many residents as Colorado.) Meanwhile, the Vermont State Police Department paid its new recruits a starting salary of about $36,700.

SALARIES FOR SUPPORT STAFF

Unsurprisingly, salary ranges for nonsworn support employees are typically lower than for sworn officers. For example, the U.S. Bureau of Labor Statistics reported in its *Occupational Outlook Handbook, 2010–11 Edition*, that as of 2008 the **median** annual wage for parking enforcement workers across the country was $32,390, although the full range was from $20,510 to more than $50,470, depending on circumstances. Meanwhile, across the United States, in 2008 correctional officers and jailers were paid a median wage of $38,380, with the lowest entry-level positions earning about $25,000.

Support employees who work part-time or on–call are typically paid by the hour. For example, a general figure for part-time translators in 2011 was about $20 per hour, with the rate rising to $30 per hour for late-night call-outs. Generally, translators are paid a minimum of two hours' pay, even if the actual work time is less.

Other support jobs offer their own salary ranges. In 2011 an evidence custodian (someone who safeguards crime evidence) for the Arizona Department of Public Safety earned about $33,400 a year, a fingerprint technician for the same agency was paid slightly more, about $33,800, and the agency's photographic specialists (who take and develop still photos at crime scenes and elsewhere) were paid about $39,200.

BENEFITS

In addition to salary, law enforcement agencies offer their officers and support staff a wide range of benefits. As is true for most companies and government positions, the specifics of these benefits packages depend on the number of hours the employee works. Full-time employees are typically eligible for full benefits, and part-time workers may also be eligible. Usually, contract workers (that is, those paid hourly or who have temporary positions) do not get benefits.

Probably the most important aspects of a benefits package lie in the health insurance plans offered to employees and their families. Some health insurance plans cover medical expenses completely, including dental and eye exams; others pay a large portion of the costs related to medical issues. Health insurance is a major part of anyone's budget, so a good health plan is an important part of any benefits package. Most agencies offer life insurance coverage as well, to provide compensation for families in the event of the employee's death.

Benefits packages also include other important forms of compensation. For example, you will be eligible for disability pay if you are injured on the job and need time to recover, or if you have an injury that qualifies you for compensation beyond what you might receive from the state. Chances are the agency will also give you hazard pay if you undertake an especially dangerous job. Furthermore, you will get a certain number of annual sick leave days and paid vacation time. Assurance of receiving disability pay and being able to take time off are especially important employment benefits in a high-pressure and sometimes dangerous job like that of a law enforcement officer.

Many agencies offer maternity leave for new mothers. Another program, generally termed "compassionate leave," enables you to take extended time off for reasons such as illness or to care for an ill or elderly relative. Some compassionate leave programs work by letting employees donate some of their own sick days or vacation time to colleagues with special needs.

Many law enforcement agencies also give you permission to supplement your basic salary by taking another job—for example, working during your off hours as a uniformed security guard at events such as concerts. Furthermore, agencies will almost always offer extra pay for overtime work. Extra pay is usually available if you work a shift that is considered less attractive (notably the "graveyard shift" in the middle of the night). Traditionally, unions have negotiated such benefits for their members.

The benefits package that an agency will offer you includes a number of long-range plans as well. Among these are pension plans, which typically let you retire in twenty or thirty years with half-pay. (However, many law enforcement agencies across the country have been facing the prospect of diminished pension plans because of overall budget cuts.) Another part of a standard benefits package is a savings plan to help you wisely conserve and invest your income.

MORE BENEFITS

Still another benefit is the chance to make your schedule as flexible as possible. This benefit, however, tends to be available mainly to employees with some seniority. Especially when they are new to a force, officers and support staff generally have little control over shift assignments.

On the other hand, many agencies have policies that allow you to adapt your weekly schedule to fit your individual needs better. Flex-time (as it is often called) lets you work the required number of hours on a nonstandard schedule. For example, instead of working a standard eight-hour shift, five days a week, you might want to be on duty for four ten-hour shifts. Of course, this would mean that your shifts were more tiring. On the other hand, such an arrangement would give you three-day weekends.

Education also figures into many benefits packages. Some law enforcement agencies accept as officers men and women with only a high school diploma or equivalent. However, if you want to be considered for promotion to the next step, sergeant, you will need more education. Typically, this means at least a two-year associate degree from a community college.

So it is clearly in your interest to advance your education. It is also in the interest of the organization—better educated employees will almost certainly be better officers. This is true not only if you obtain a college degree, but also if you attend training sessions or seminars on topics such as advanced firearms techniques. Typically, the agency you work for will pay for these classes.

To encourage officers and staffers to improve their qualifications, many agencies will assist you with educational costs. They may help you pay for tuition and other fees if you are taking classes related to your work. They might also arrange for you to have time off, or change your work hours to fit your class schedule.

Agencies typically offer many more benefits to attract good employees. For example, most law enforcement agencies provide their officers and uniformed support staff with yearly allowances for purchasing uniforms and keeping them clean. Furthermore, daily **stipends** to pay for meals and other job-related expenses are often included. Other benefits can include paid health club memberships, which benefit the department as well as individuals, since regular workouts keep employees in top physical shape. Furthermore, agencies typically organize events such as picnics, sports leagues, and parties to help employees and their families bond and to encourage them to befriend one another.

As an officer or support staff employee in a city, county, or state police agency, you will be well paid—especially if it is your first job after high school or college. And you will have many other benefits, such as health plans, as well. Still, the first and foremost benefit to any job in law enforcement will always be a sense of personal satisfaction and fulfillment. You will know that you are doing a vital job—helping your community in real ways and keeping its citizens safe from harm.

GLOSSARY

cadet—A student at a law enforcement academy.

custodial—Relating to protective actions, such as guarding detainees.

evidence technician—A forensic specialist who collects and catalogs evidence from a crime or accident scene.

GED—General Educational Development (also called a General Education Diploma or General Equivalency Diploma), a series of tests that results in a diploma equivalent to a high school degree. The GED is typically taken by people who, for whatever reason, have not graduated from a standard high school.

incorporated—Not legally united as a single urban center. Typically, a sheriff's office is responsible for those regions of its county that are not incorporated as towns or cities.

jurisdiction—The region, such as a city, county, or state, in which an organization has legal authority; in the case of a law enforcement agency, this authority includes arresting and detaining criminal suspects.

K-9—A law enforcement unit that uses specially trained dogs (canines) to detect explosives or drugs, or to search for fugitives or missing persons.

median—The middle of a range of numbers.

polygraph test—A means of generating a record that will enable analysts to evaluate the truthfulness of a person's responses to questions.

rookie—A beginner, such as a new law enforcement officer.

sequestered—Kept away from contact with others, as when members of a jury must be prevented from being influenced by anything outside the courtroom.

stipend—A set amount of money provided by one's employer for daily expenses, such as meals and travel.

sworn officer—A law enforcement employee who has taken an oath of office, and thus has the full authority to make arrests and undertake all other duties of an officer.

CAREERS IN STATE, COUNTY, AND CITY POLICE FORCES

NOTES

INTRODUCTION

p. 6, "Once, on a traffic stop . . . ": Trooper Shelley Izzard, Michigan State Police, interview with author, 2/19/11.

p. 7, "It can be . . . ": Sgt J. J. Gundermann, Washington State Patrol, interview with author, 2/14/11.

p. 10, "Eight hours . . . ": Senior Officer Mike McCoy, Houston (TX) Police Department, interview with author, 2/16/11.

p. 11, "You're driving . . . ": Trooper Shelley Izzard, Michigan State Police, interview with author, 2/19/11.

CHAPTER 1

p. 15, "[Y]ou get . . . ": Deputy David D. Peterson, Benton County (OR) Sheriff's Office, interview with author, 2/15/11.

p. 17, "It's very simple . . . ": Senior Officer Mike McCoy, Houston (TX) Police Department, interview with author, 2/16/11.

p. 18, "A big part . . . ": School Resource Officer Jennifer Williamson, Orlando (FL) Police Department, interview with author, 2/11/11.

p. 20, "You've got . . . ": Sgt J. J. Gundermann, Washington State Patrol, interview with author, 2/14/11.

p. 20–21, "It does . . . ": Deputy David D. Peterson, Benton County (OR) Sheriff's Office, interview with author, 2/15/11.

p. 21, "The biggest . . . ": Officer Adam Elias, Seattle (WA) Police Department, interview with author, 3/1/11.

p. 22, "One out of twenty . . . ": Senior Officer Mike McCoy, Houston (TX) Police Department, interview with author, 2/16/11.

p. 24–25, "It used to be . . . ": Trooper Shelley Izzard, Michigan State Police, interview with author, 2/19/11.

p. 26, "Pay attention . . . ": Senior Officer Mike McCoy, Houston (TX) Police Department, interview with author, 2/16/11.

p. 28, "Definitely if you're bilingual . . . ": Dispatcher Leslie Lugo, Dutchess County (NY) Sheriff's Office, interview with author, 2/17/11.

NOTES

p. 29, "We are . . . ": Matthew Kemeny, "Some midstate police departments still struggle with minority hires, mayor says." *Patriot-News* (central PA), July 13, 2009, www.pennlive.com/ midstate/index.ssf/2009/07/some_midstate_police_ departmen.html

CHAPTER 2

p. 32, "My class . . . ": Trooper Shelley Izzard, Michigan State Police, interview with author, 2/19/11.

p. 33, "Every person . . . ": Sgt J. J. Gundermann, Washington State Patrol, interview with author, 2/14/11.

p. 34, "Every trooper . . . " Sgt J. J. Gundermann, Washington State Patrol, interview with author, 2/14/11.

p. 34, "A lot . . . ": Senior Officer Mike McCoy, Houston (TX) Police Department, interview with author, 2/16/11.

p. 37, "In the academy . . . ": Senior Officer Mike McCoy, Houston (TX) Police Department, interview with author, 2/16/11.

p. 40, "At first . . . ": Officer Adam Elias, Seattle (WA) Police Department, interview with author, 3/1/11.

p. 42, "Our graduation . . . ": Trooper Shelley Izzard, Michigan State Police, interview with author, 2/19/11.

p. 43, "I went through . . . ": School Resource Officer Jennifer Williamson, Orlando (FL) Police Department, interview with author, 2/11/11.

p. 44, "On my honor . . .": Dan Rodricks, "Honor is not for cowards," *Baltimore Sun*, March 1, 2011, http://articles.baltimoresun.com/2011-03-01/news/ bal-rodricks-column0301_1_honor-younger-cops-majestic

p. 44–45, "I didn't . . . ": Dispatcher Leslie Lugo, Dutchess County (NY) Sheriff's Office, interview with author, 2/17/11.

CHAPTER 4

p. 62, "After the academy . . .": Officer Adam Elias, Seattle (WA) Police Department, interview with author, 3/1/11.

p. 64, "You kind of . . . ": Sgt J. J. Gundermann, Washington State Patrol, interview with author, 2/14/11.

p. 66, "I sometimes feel . . . ": Dispatcher Leslie Lugo, Dutchess County (NY) Sheriff's Office, interview with author, 2/17/11.

CHAPTER 5

p. 82, "For example, the U.S. . . . ": U.S. Department of Labor, *Occupational Outlook Handbook 2010–2011 Edition* (New York: Skyhorse, 2010).

FURTHER INFORMATION

BOOKS

Allman, Toney. *Crime Scene Investigations: The Homicide Detective.* Farmington Hills, MI: Lucent Press, 2009.

Field, Shelly. *Ferguson Career Coach: Managing Your Career in Law Enforcement.* New York: Chelsea House, 2008.

Newton, Michael. *The Texas Rangers.* New York: Chelsea House, 2010.

Worth, Richard. *Los Angeles Police Department.* New York: Chelsea House, 2010.

WEBSITES

Bureau of Labor Statistics, "Police and Detectives."
www.bls.gov/oco/ocos160.htm
This site, maintained by the U.S. Department of Labor, has extensive information on careers in law enforcement.

Legal Careers, "8 Hot Jobs in Law Enforcement."
http://legalcareers.about.com/od/careerprofiles/tp/Law-Enforcement-Careers.htm

Netsmart Workshop, "Teens" and "Law Enforcement."
www.netsmartz.org/Teens
These pages, part of a site maintained by the National Center for Missing and Exploited Children, have videos and more about law enforcement agencies and other subjects such as cyber-bullying.

BIBLIOGRAPHY

ARTICLES

Kemeny, Matthew. "Some midstate police departments still struggle with minority hires, mayor says." *Patriot-News* (central PA), July 13, 2009, www.pennlive.com/midstate/index.ssf/2009/07/some_midstate_police_department.html

Rodricks, Dan. "Honor is not for cowards." *Baltimore Sun*, March 1, 2011, http://articles.baltimoresun.com/2011-03-01/news/bal-rodricks-column0301_1_honor-younger-cops-majestic

INTERVIEWS

Deputy Sheriff David D. Peterson, Benton County (Oregon) Sheriff's Office, February 15, 2011.

Dispatcher Leslie Lugo, Dutchess County (New York) Sheriff's Office, February 17, 2011.

Officer Adam Elias, Seattle (Washington) Police Department, March 3, 2011.

Officer Jennifer Williamson, Orange County (Florida) Sheriff's Office, February 11, 2011.

Senior Officer Mike McCoy, Houston (Texas) Police Department, February 16, 2011.

Sergeant J. J. Gundermann, Washington State Patrol, February 14, 2011.

Trooper Shelley Izzard, Michigan State Police, February 19, 2011.

INDEX

Page numbers in **boldface** are illustrations.

INDEX

INDEX

ABOUT THE AUTHOR

ADAM WOOG is the author of many books for adults, young adults, and children. His most recent books are *Military Might and Global Intervention* in the Controversy! series, and the five other titles in this series. Woog lives in his hometown of Seattle, Washington, with his wife. Their daughter, a college student, is majoring in criminal justice and criminology.